The Alarm Clock

The Essence of Moving in Silence

Darrell Q. Slade

Darrell Q. Slade

ISBN: 1973851350
ISBN-13: 978-1973851356

DEDICATION

This Book is dedicated to Darrell Louise Slade and Jackie Jordan

HOPE

Hope frees your mind of reality. Hope is the cousin of faith. Where does hope come from? Hope is that vision embedded in the back of your head that's destined to be released to the world. Yeah, it maybe farfetched but why is it there? Hope is a preview of the movie God scripted for your life.

Prologue

Most people believe change is easy but it requires great sacrifice and courage. Our society today is comfortable. We don't want to move from the position we are in because we fear what we may lose: a job, money, feelings, friends. Attachments are cancer, eating away our hope. That's why there isn't much change in the world. The politicians can't do it, the preachers can't do it, the focal groups can't do it— it happens with inside you.

The systems today in America are road blocks; they serve no true purpose. Yet we invest all our hope in these elected individuals when the same shit has been happening for ages. Nothing has changed.

Psychological Slavery is a mindset, far worse than what our ancestors encountered. Our abstract values are our most treasured assets. The craziness in the world we live in forces those jewels to be oppressed.

This book is a call for change. We have to change the way we think. We have to change the moves we make. Instead of building another man's kingdom, we need to build our own. We have an equivalent amount of power as human beings but you can't attain your innate abilities until you set your mind free.

Take this journey with me and free your mind of the norms as you learn my deepest thoughts. I open myself up in this book because I can't make a call for change without being truthful. I'm a very introverted person. I don't share my thoughts with everyone, but God called me to send this message to his people through this book. Therefore I put my ego aside and was obedient.

I'm not in this for profit, it's about the bigger picture, I am a humanist not a capitalist. If you told me five years ago that I would write and publish my own book at twenty-two, I would say you need to see a psychiatrist. Pride can be a hindrance. Had I not humbled myself, this book would not have been written.

We all experience what I refer to as a *dark cloud* in life. I would like to walk you through my obstacles and the endurance it took to overcome them.

I was very strategic when I wrote The Alarm Clock. I pray that you can truly grasp the message that I am trying to get through. I do not want to categorize this book as religious because by no means am I religious, but very spiritual. Religion is just another form of segregation. You see, we are all one—the children of God.

Religion, race, capitalism, separation of power, social class— all blocks us from humanity. We need unity!

The Alarm Clock is a wakeup call, a message that needs to be heard. Too many people are asleep, living in darkness. Someone needs to come with that light; like when your parents opens the blinds in the morning and the sunlight bursts through, forcing you to wake up!

We all have an alarm clock. Allow me to explain.

I

"Whoever cannot seek the unforeseen *sees nothing* for the known way is an impasse." -Heraclitus

Before I was born, my mother was told it was merely impossible for her to ever conceive a child again.

My father, Gordon Slade, served in the Navy during the Vietnam War. While stationed in Long Beach, California, he had his first child Kera Slade by a woman named Shirley Dale. After Kera was born my father moved to Vallejo, outside of San Francisco, where he married his first wife Sandra Kay. They gave birth to Tina Kay Slade in 1974. After Tina was born, they moved to Winston-Salem, North Carolina. Ten years later my father and Sandra Kay had their second daughter, Jessica. Soon after Jessica was born their marriage was short lived.

My mother, Darrell Louise Jones was born on March 22nd, 1951 in Louisville, Kentucky. Hair was her passion, she worked at multiple salons, in Louisville. When she was twenty-three she had her first son Carlos Jones. In the early eighties her and Carlos relocated to Winston-Salem.

When my mother moved to Winston she met my father at a church she attended called St. Peters. Six months after they met, they decided to jump the broom. Around this same time, Carlos's father, Winnie, was killed in Kentucky. This made it difficult for Carlos to accept his new "step-father". As you could imagine the household was very blended. Jessica and Tina spent most of their time with their mother and Kera only lived in North Carolina for one year when she was thirteen.

My mom opened her own Salon in Winston,

Darrell's Salon of Beauty, and became a well-known hair dresser in the area, her most profound customer was Dr. Maya Angelou.

In the early nineties my mother was invited to a national hair show in Atlanta; she took my father with her to the hair convention that year. While they were there, they went shopping Lennox Mall, a popular mall in Atlanta.

At the mall, my mother noticed a tall, slim, light skinned fella in his early to mid-twenties. "Look!", she told my father, "There's our son!". My father looked at her as if she was crazy, "What are you talking about, Darrell?" he asked. "Our son! God showed him to me! That's him!". This was around the time the doctors was telling her it was impossible for her to have another child. My mother was a woman of faith, she knew God was trying to send her a message.

If my mother believed what the doctors told her, I'd doubt I would be here. But God works in mysterious ways, he can perform the *unforeseen.*

When God shows you something, even if it seems impossible, you have to believe it and it will happen.

A couple of years later, on January 26, 1995, my mother gave birth to me. I was nine pounds and eight ounces. We had a special bond since that moment. I was the apple of her eye.

God gave my mother a vision, yes it seemed impossible but he stayed true to his word. My mother was forty-three when she birthed me which is rare, but God made a way.

When I turned of age, my mother sacrificed doing hair to invest more time with me in school and sports. Hair was her passion, but I was her priority. This was the sweetest thing she ever did for me. I value every moment spent with her.

In March of 2008, my moms got real sick. The doctors told her she had to take off from work. My ma was a healthy woman, she always took care of her body, so I wasn't sure how she got ill.

When she first got sick, she asked me to read her a scripture from the Bible. The scripture I chose was Galatians 5:22, *the fruit of the spirit.* This was one of the few scriptures I knew off the top of my head.

Galatians 5:22-23 KJV

But the fruit of the Spirit is love, joy, peace, longsuffering, gentleness, goodness, faith, meekness, temperance: against such thing there is no law.

I had no clue what that scripture meant, I was just doing what my mother asked. After I read it, she hugged me real tight, those words spoke to her more than I realized.

Things started to go downhill from there. She was out of work longer than expected and was in and out of the hospital periodically. I was oblivious to the whole situation. Over the summer she lost all her hair to chemo-therapy. As an optimist, I tried to think positive, but it killed me seeing my mother like that. I never asked her what was going on I just made sure I stayed by her side. During this period, my mom endured a lot of pain, but she stayed strong for me. She didn't want me to know what was going on because of the impact it would have on me.

My mom didn't inform me of her situation until January of the following year; she had just got her breast removed and was going through, emotionally. She called me into her bedroom and explained to me that she had a rare form of cancer. The cancer developed in her back and spread to her breast which is why she had to get her breast removed. Despite it all, she told me that things were going to get better and for me to stay strong for her.

Everyday my mother would have to go to chemotherapy and either my brother or my cousin, Shawn, would take her. I was a knuckle head in school and would always get suspended. In fact, I spent my birthday on suspension. My mother was upset with me as any parent would be with their child. However, I had an opportunity to spend more time with her around the house while I was suspended, this was bittersweet. Ultimately, I felt like I wasn't helping her situation, instead, making it worse.

One day, my brother came to take her to chemo. She told me she would be back within an hour. Instead of coming home after her appointment, she was sent to the hospital. That hour then turned into days, days into weeks— this was very frustrating, I just wanted my mother healed.

When I would go visit her at the hospital— she'd asked me to push her around the hallways in her wheelchair; this gave her a reason to get out of the room and for us to spend quality time together. My mother loved my company. One morning while I was there, she had a few visitors up to see her, she asked me to read what then became her favorite scripture *Galatians 5:22*. I believe hearing me read that was like a remedy to her. After I read the scripture she told me, in a calm yet joyful voice, that she was proud of me. This meant a lot especially after all I put her through.

Finally, I got the news that she would be coming home within a week. I was excited like a kid on Christmas for she had been gone for nearly three weeks.

That next day, my father called and told me that instead of her coming home, she would have to go to the hospice. I was extremely upset when I got the news. The Hospice is a center where immediate care is needed at all times.

When I went to school the next day, no one could grasp what was wrong with me, quite frankly I didn't feel like talking to anyone. My teacher sent me to the office, and called my brother. Carlos was the only person who could simmer my frustration. Once they figured out why I was upset, they asked if I wanted to speak to my mother whom they had called over the phone, **I regrettably said no**.

I went home early that day with my brother. We went to the park and had a long conversation about our mom, we agreed to stay positive and trusted God would see us through the situation. This uplifted my spirit.

The following day, **February 27th**, started off well. I was in a better mood after the conversation with my brother plus I had a lot to look forward to. My good friends and I were in a talent show that evening. We were going to perform Soulja Boy *Turn my swag on*, a popular song at the time.

My last class of the day was 8th grade literature. My teacher, Mrs. Elson, was extremely hard on me only because she knew my potential. My goal was to stay out of trouble.

I made it through the day with no phone calls or write ups, everything was going smooth. Then the phone rang. I had a feeling it was for me. In the back of my head I was thinking *what now? this can't be real*, but it was. I had been called up to the office.

Anticipation stirred as I made my way to the office. The first person I saw in the office was my basketball coach he said "you stay up here don't you?!". The receptionist told me that I wasn't in trouble; my sister, Tina, had come to get me and my nephew, Trentan. Trentan was Tina's first born, we were two weeks apart and lived together for majority of our childhood.

I was confused to why Tina was getting us out of school early, but I was more upset than anything. All the talent show participants were required to stay after school that evening; I stressed that to Tina, but she insisted that we needed to go see my mother. I told her that I planned to go see her afterwards, but Tina said she wasn't leaving without us. I didn't want to cause a big scene, so we left.

The car ride to the hospice was quite odd. The whole time I was thinking why would Tina randomly come get us but I refrained from asking any questions, so we were quiet the whole way. Nonetheless I was happy to see my mother because I hadn't seen her in three days and I knew she was ready to see me.

My mom always had a bright smile that electrified the room when I would go see her. That smile always brought me much joy.

When we pulled up to the hospice. My father was standing at the side door entrance. I was extremely puzzled. The first thing my father said to me struck me like lightning, it wasn't *hey how was school* or *glad y'all made it here safe,* the usual greeting a father would give his son. Instead he informed me that my mother had died.

Just like that the woman who sacrificed so much for her child, that wasn't supposed to be born, was gone. It wasn't until that moment where I discovered how powerful words could be. I didn't want to believe what my father had told me. I lost control of my body as if a piece of me died. Tears instantly began to rush down my face. One sentence changed my life forever!

I went three days without seeing my mother and the next time I would walk in her room she wouldn't be smiling. The day prior, I had the opportunity to speak with her over the phone, that was the last chance I'd ever get to hear her voice, that kills my soul even to this day. I didn't have the courage to go see her after I found out the news. My cousin, Maria, had to convince me to go in the room.

Witnessing my mother lay there was the worst sight I've ever seen, her mouth was open and looked as if she had a peaceful transition, but she didn't leave peace behind. I couldn't help but to holler as if I had broken my arm or something of that nature. My father told me that before she passed, her last words were *everything will be alright.* That was hard for me to comprehend because things only got worse. I slowly approached her and gave her one last kiss on the forehead.

A child's relationship with their mother is incomparable to any other relationship. No child should have to experience losing a mother at an early age.

Oddly enough, I wanted to go to the talent show

that evening. I felt like I owed it to the crowd and especially my boys, I didn't want to let them down. I told them that my mom had passed, they were understanding and said we didn't have to perform, but I wanted to speak. Quite frankly, I didn't know what I was doing. I never liked talking in front of large crowds, but I felt this was something I had to do. When I got up there I was at peace. I informed the crowd of my situation then thanked everyone, in the crowd that evening, who supported my mother. I don't know how I had the strength to do that, my heart was so weak. That was the strongest thing I probably ever did throughout my lifetime.

When my mom died, the family died, this killed my joy. I was bitter. She was the nucleus that kept the family together. My mom always preached how we how we must stay together as family. But after she passed, my family just took that message and threw it down the drain. I tried my best to continue my mother's legacy and keep my family together but some things can't be fixed.

This situation prepared me for the life ahead of me, the good and the bad.

II

"I need a new nigga, for this black cloud I follow cause while it's over me it's too dark to see tomorrow." –Nas *Illmatic*

February 27th, 2009— was dark, cold, and rainy. That forecast symbolizes my life ever since that very day. Losing a mother paralyzes a son indelibly. My mother meant the world to me. I remember one night, as a kid, I was waiting for my ma to come home from the beauty salon, I began to think *what would I do if my mother never came home? What would I do without her?* Having answered those questions is something that I wish on nobody, not even my worse enemies. I never thought I would lose my mom.

Everybody knew except for me and my brother. We were under the impression that she was about to come home. I cleaned the house vividly because she had been gone for almost a month and I wanted her to come to refreshing home. No one wanted, my brother and I, to know that those were her last days. This was painful, I didn't find out until recently, eight years later. Had we known we could've spent more intimate time with our mother. I yearn for those moments because we don't have that anymore and growing up we rarely had those times where it was just us three— me, my brother and ma. I can have it spiritually, and mentally I can reflect.

Having your mom in your life for fourteen years and then to lose her forever, automatically produces a *dark cloud.*

My home was empty. I didn't know who to trust, the world was cold and lonely— that's not a good feeling. Losing a mother ain't easy, it feels like I was diagnosed, after she left, with an eternal sickness. I been in this world alone since I was fourteen. I hate even typing this piece right now because it reminds me of that day. I would always cover that pain away. Because I was told *you can't always use that as an excuse Q!* but damn near every day is tough for me. I can't call her in the evening and tell her about my day or talk with her about my deepest emotions. It's a nightmare, I wake up with the chills in the middle of the night. Back then I didn't care to go to college or to finish high school.

Losing a loved one makes you look at life differently. I never really understood how I pushed through after that day. Eventually, I had to realize that I can't let pain stop me, I had to keep moving forward. Life goes on!

My life hasn't been the same since I lost my mother. Things that make other people happy aren’t as gratifying to me, things that bring joy to others aren't as appealing. Accomplishments simmer well with most people but not me. I feel like a piece of me is missing. This has been a struggle for me.

Thinking back to that time when my wound was fresh, I was immature. I got caught up with the wrong crowds. I tried slinging dope, I indulged into fights, skipped school, smoked, you name it— I was headed down the path of destruction.

My freshman year in high school I attended North Forsyth, I was so bad that they literately were about to send me to the alternative school, Griffith. I remember one instance where I left school, mid-day, came back high and got busted. I ain't care.

Most people get involved with those things because that's the lifestyle that they are brought up in, others do it to be cool, for me it was a cover-up to hide the pain that I was enduring. I was a lost soul. There were nights where I would walk for miles just to cope. Dark clouds seeps from hell to dim the light from above.

When I was lost and going down the wrong paths my mother's words began to dwell on me, *I'm proud of you son.* I asked myself what was I doing to truly make my mother proud. Nothing! I heard her speak to me, spiritually and she said: *this isn't the path God destined for you, this isn't you*! Moving forward, I had to change my surroundings, this wasn't easy, but I had to do it. I went to a whole new school and had I not made those changes, I don't know where I would've been today, damn sure wouldn't be writing this book.

It requires change for you to grow. I changed everything, I started hanging around people who were inspired to go to college and were eager to be somebody in life. This motivated me, it gave me hope. But at the same time, I was still lost because I was a motherless child. This is very painful, but it's a part of life.

Your loved ones may not be there with you physically along your journey, hardships are inevitable, but that isn't a reason to give up.

I wish every day that my mother was here. I

wanted her at my graduation ceremonies and my high school proms and football games. Before she passed it got to a point where she told me *I don't even care if you graduated anymore,* she was that frustrated with me because I was a troublesome child.

Unfortunately, she passed three months before my eighth-grade graduation, so she wasn't there to see me graduate. I barely made it to graduation, I had been expelled three weeks prior, but somehow, the school allowed me to walk. This was a symbolic moment— I wanted my mom there to show her, this is the future, a new beginning!

What changed my life was picking up the word of God; that's what gave me light when I was at the lowest moments in my life. The word won't mean anything to you if you never been through anything. When you are empty those words become powerful because it fills you up— this is what the Bible did for me. Everything that I'm saying is genuine, it gives light because it comes from the source. The word shows your path. God was saying *I still have a path for you, it's going to be a rocky road, but it's destined for you to travel.*

Everyone has a dark cloud that seeps in their life at some point, it may not be as tragic as losing a mother, or it could be worst. Clouds are constantly moving, they do not remain stagnant in, so don't lose hope when a dark clouds seeps into your life. A cloud's purpose, is to produce rain to allow things such as plants to grow and have life. Those plants would not have life if not those dark clouds passed through.

Notice the plant on the book cover; that's the tree of life in its early stages!

When a dark cloud enters our life it's an opportunity for growth. Real growth happens in darkness. Throughout your journey, you are going to encounter some dark paths, but you have to be willing to have the courage to embrace them. The apostle James wrote *we should be of great joy when we face hardships because it's an opportunity to grow our endurance*. You can't battle through life without endurance, or else when the winds blow your foundation will be knocked down.

Had I not lost my mother I don't think I would've matured as much. Granted I yearn for her presence every day. But those hardships I faced early on matured, I was stronger mentally. I feel like I've been isolated since fourteen. My dad was always there and despite our differences, he helped me a lot, I'll always appreciate him for that. However, it was up to me to make something out of my life and it was my mother's words that gave me the courage to do that.

I was complacent growing up, came from a good home with both parents. My mother tried her best to keep me away from the things that she witnessed growing up, she wanted me to have a good life. This only made me unappreciative, I took life for granted, I was always doing stupid shit. Sometimes I believe God intentionally causes something tragic for us to wake up.

As I grew older I began to understand that it was

my mother's time to go. I realize that she is in a better place now, suffering no more, free of the worldly craziness. Now she is free, at peace, filled with joy in unison with the lord in the kingdom of heaven. Her lost made me stronger!

III

"This guy had slave on his face. You think he wanted the masters with his masters?" -Jay Z 4:44

Abraham Lincoln did not free the slaves during the Emancipation Proclamation— it's a myth! Lincoln's Emancipation order only applied to the slaves that were in Rebellion against the United States. "Slavery didn't end" until three years later when the thirteenth amendment was ratified yet a hundred and fifty years later, in America, we're still enslaved!

The chains aren't metal anymore they are mental, it's a mindset, a system— economics. Slaves today don't realize they're oppressed. Our people feel defeated

because we are black. That's what they have us thinking, that's what they want us to think— it's all a distraction. Half of its true though. In the eighties, Reagan flooded crack cocaine into the projects.
"*Crime increased, death rates increased, and our people became complacent— subjected to the system. Incarceration rates in the United States were sky high. The United States imprisons more people than any other "autocratic" country. White folks used and sold crack more than the black people— somehow the black people went to prison for it. Our prison population grew more than nine hundred percent. The war on drugs began in 1971. The prison population was two hundred thousand now it is over two million.*" -Shawn Carter on The War on Drugs

Our low-income communities have invisible barriers, no defined walls, but we fear to go past because we feel it is impossible to withhold what's on the outside, when in all reality we can! This was all a strategic move, it's psychological. *If you think you are beaten you are*, it's all in your mind. We don't have to be subjected to the system, it damn sure cant interfere with our path in life unless we allow it to. The key is to believe but most importantly faith. Faith is strategic, you'll have to develop short-term goals to accomplish whatever you have faith in. If you believe in something don't let anything sway you from it.

Obama told his self that he was going to become President of the United States, imagine how many people doubted him, *A black man? As president? In the US? - Nah.* But he proved the critics wrong but more so, he proved his self right.

Faith and believing are the pathways to the Underground Railroad that will lead to your freedom. Not believing is slavery within its self, you are holding yourself captive. The unique thing about faith is can't nobody take that shit away from you! The man above said that we are here to inherit the Earth and everything that's in it, it's ours! So, who is the next man to tell you what you can or can't do?

Escape with the mentality of Nat Turner and free

your mind. Once you become free it's a great feeling, almost like when you make it to the mountaintop and look out into the world and began to realize that it is all your inheritance. When you operate in faith you began to manifest what God has blessed you with plus dividends, your cup will overflow.

You don't have to be in a system, you can create your own! Creativity is being able to develop your own empire and release it to the world. If there's no creativity there's complacency, lukewarm, mediocracy. Why settle when you're destined build your own empire?

You construct your own path. Gifted people are giving all their talents to a system whose manipulating them. It takes a huge sacrifice to be free. If you focus on your gift to the world, you can use that to create an empire, for yourself. Whether it's sports, art, music, writing, etc. All it takes is dedication! Starting off is the hardest part but once you have the establishment, you can level up. This is our calling.

The culture would shift, if everyone embraced their gifts and shared it willingly to the world. Picture a society where students get law degrees to start their own law institutes, providing top tier courses for kids who can't afford to get an education or who weren't accepted by elite universities; or finance majors, developing their own ventured capital fund that invests in low income communities, elevating that environment. This would have a huge social and economic impact. *Buy back the block.* There's a lot more I want to say on this subject but I'll save for my next novel— *there's a time and place for everything.*

Instead of holding our hands up saying *don't shoot,* we need to create our own shit! That's unexpected, especially from the black community. They expect us to riot and destroy our neighborhoods, they expect us to kill each other, and deteriorate our minds (our holy tabernacles), because of drug abuse, "it's a project", get it? We as a culture need to become one with the universe, when youre in sync with the universe nothing can oppress you.

An educated black man poses a threat to society, that's why they try to keep us away from the table. That's why during the time of slavery it was unlawful for a slave to learn how to read and write. Same shit is happening today, just coded differently, it's "unlawful" for a black person to create their own shit. That's why they tried to keep us in the projects or why we can only go but so far up that corporate latter. They love you when you are in their system, but they hate you when you break loose! We are Gods not slaves, peace.

The world is ours! They tell us that we can't have this, or we can't have that. That's what they tell you and you going to believe they? Who are they? You telling me you believe in they? That's who you believe in? When they taking all your money, they confining you in the projects, they use you as an experiment, they give you the bare minimum of their profit. They got government welfare, but they are eating good. They on flights sponsored by the government but you struggle to fill your tank up because inflation and massive oil prices that they benefit from. They ain't got to worry about their next meal, they bellies filled with government cheese, while it's people in the same country starving but you believe in they!? So you on your ass because they said sit on your ass.

During the time of slavery, the *house niggas* were the ones who felt the freest because they had more luxury than the *field niggas,* but they were still slaves, taking orders. Nowadays the government controls the field niggas, and corporate America manipulates the house niggas— they all under one roof.

Fredrick Douglass figured it out early, he learned how to read and write by playing the white man's game, kept the knowledge secret, and used it against them. It's not a race war it's about taking what's yours even if you have to read the unwritten laws to attain it. If you aren't giving an opportunity, create one!

Society expects us to scream black lives matter, but

really all that matters is knowing that you matter. Nothing can stop you from achieving your destiny but you— not the government, not the rich folk, not even your enemies, it's you. They don't expect us to create our own shit, especially when you're in a system. That's why it's key to break free and take what's yours! If it wasn't valuable, they wouldn't keep you from it.

Alexander the Great didn't go to Egypt by chance he was in awe of the intellect of the people of melanin, so he enslaved them to grow his empire! Study the game, take it, and use it to create your own plan. Let the opponent play their cards first, watch how they deal, then you play your hand.

People now want to believe what society preaches to them. They tell us that we have to go to school and build our resumes, and get a job. Society says that if you come from a certain environment then you are going to be sub-closed to that environment forever. But when you go against the odds and take that leap, you might fail a couple of times, but you did it, you broke loose. If you keep pushing forward it's going to take you further than any system will guarantee.

My senior year of high school the odds were against me. I had been told all throughout grade school that I would be another statistic and would fall into the system, no one knew I'd go to college. This fueled my determination. I had to get to college but my discipline reports from my freshman and sophomore years were as big as a bible. On top of that my grades weren't up to par. I began making honor roll my junior year but my piss poor performance in the classroom from early on weighed down my GPA. Despite it all, I told myself that I still would apply to college. I really wanted to go to the University of North Carolina at Wilmington, thought it would be a great atmosphere, so I applied. I also applied to eight other Universities such as East Carolina, Appalachian State University, etc.

Throughout the application process, I had the opportunity to meet with the provost from Winston-Salem State University, Dr. Brenda Allen. During the meeting, she asked about my application process and if I had applied to the University, the typical conversation a faculty member would have with a graduating senior. Winston was my last school of choice, I had to get out of Winston, but I didn't tell her that. From that meeting, we formed a relationship and she told me to come meet with her again next month.

After our meeting, things began to shift downhill. I started receiving letters in the mail from the colleges that I applied to. Literally, I got denied by every single school. Once they saw my discipline report, and my GPA, there was no way they were going to accept me. I was still determined however, I had been working extremely hard to get to college. This was around the same time that I had been reading my word and learning the laws of faith. Faith is a discipline, it forces you to see things that aren't there— *The unforeseen.*

A month had passed, and I had another meeting with Dr. Allen; she followed up with me on my application process, I had to be honest with her, I told her I hadn't been accepted anywhere that I applied. At that moment something told me to ask her about Winston and I did. This was humbling for me, but her response was simple "give me your transcript and your SAT scores and I'll handle the rest." I didn't understand, how could this have been that simple. I went on to explain to her that my SATs scores and my GPA were well below the requirements she repeated herself "give me your transcript and your SAT scores and I'll handle the rest." The next few days I found out that I had been accepted.

I will always honor Dr. Allen for giving me that opportunity. This goes to show that God will reward those who are humble and have a relentless fortitude. Winston was my last option, I didn't want to go there but when a door opens, you must walk through it.

I went against the odds and because of that God made a way. When I got to college more doors began to open for me. On top of that, the HBCU experience was second to none.

Never allow your current obstacle to dictate where you go in life instead allow it to build the framework of your future. Your gifts have the power to crack through concrete and sprout a tree, filled with knowledge and fruits that will produce life for others who need it. *Hence the book cover.*

You must set yourself free! Never let society control your thoughts! Keep moving forward!

IV

"Fear what other people greed, and greed what others fear."
– Warren Buffett

Everyone wants to be successful and live the American dream, accumulating wealth and having an Estate in the Hamptons, living debt free. But everyone doesn't realize that success comes with a price.

My first real job was a "Customer Service Associate" for the Winston-Salem Dash, a local minor league baseball team. Really, I was a janitor, emptying trash cans, cleaning out bathrooms, sweeping trash after customers. *I hated it.* This was humbling but made me appreciate work. This was my first job, so I was grateful but at the same time I knew that wasn't my end goal.

While I was at work I would always have conversations with the peanut man, and if you're from Winston you know who I'm referring too. I respect this man, he is ambitious, humble, and has a very successful business. One day, I told him *I can't be here long, God has something better for me.* He told me something that would stick, **the reward for hard work is more hard work.**

To make it to the top you must make a sacrifice and be willing to work even harder.

Circumcision is painful. Especially when you don't get circumcised during birth. As humans it's easy for us to get attached to things: sex, drugs, relationships, or doesn't even have to be a concrete object. It can be fear, doubt, strife, jealousy, depression, anger— you name it! But where God is taking you, those attachments can't go, therefore you have to let them go. The longer we allow things to sit in our lives the more painful it will be when we cut it out.

The Bible talks about this in Joshua chapter five.

After Moses, God put Joshua in charge to lead his people, the Israelites, to the promised land. Moses had delivered the Israelites from slavery in Egypt. God promised them a land filled with milk and honey, this indicates a land of success. We each have a land God promised us, it's our vision, our destiny, our calling—our alarm clocks. We all are on a journey to that land. The journey is just as important as the destination. Trust the process!

Right before Josh and the Israelites entered the promised land, they ran into a huge road block, the wall of Jericho. We all have roadblocks that we encounter on our voyage in life. God said to Joshua, tell your men to march around that wall seven times and on the seventh time, shout as loud as you can. But before you begin to march make sure all the men are circumcised. A circumcision as an adult hurts far worse than it would had they been circumcised at childbirth. God says that the circumcision will prepare them for battle. He is asking us to do the same, not literally, but there are certain things that we must cut out our lives to move forward. Notice God asked a task that seemed to not make sense, but Joshua remained obedient and because of that God fulfilled his promise. On the seventh time around, the men shouted because of the faith they had, and the wall tumbled down. When we began to see the vision, God has for us, we too will began to shout with joy and that destroys any obstacle that interferes with our path.

Making it to the promised land is joyful but it is also painful because of the sacrifices you had to make to get there. You may have to cut a friend, you may have to cut comfortability, you may be in an unhealthy relationship, but what God has in store for you is far greater than what you're leaving behind. You must be obedient and discipline, but most importantly you must have the wisdom to comprehend.

Sometimes you'll have to cut those narrow-minded individuals who don't see nor comprehend your vision. They too are a distraction and will have you believing everything they say. Stay away from average people, they can become a cancer. Keep greatness within your circle because it's contagious.

When I got to college I had a lot of freedom. Freedom can be a distraction too. When you're exposed to freedom you get tempted. I began to lose focus in college. There's nothing wrong with enjoying your college experience; partying, chasing women, pledging, etc. but it can get you off track if you allow it to. It's extremely important to have discipline. Discipline will keep you in line with your vision when you are tempted to procrastinate.

Wisdom reveals, in order to grow you have to have a circumcision, which isn't easy to adapt to. I had certain things that I had to cut out my life during undergrad—not saying that it was easy, we all are far from perfect, but this indeed was resourceful and kept me focused.

A quote I live by

"Live like no one else so later in life you can live like no one else." –Dave Ramsey

Enjoy your life but remember your call of duty and don't lose sight of it. **If we are living life differently from the crowd, we will soon be above the crowd**.

Nothing can grow if there is no pressure being applied. The Israelites were in an uncomfortable pain when they had to march around the walls of Jericho. Be joyful when pressure is applied for it is an opportunity for growth.

Warren Buffet says he'll never invest in a company that has never failed. Knowledge is produced when you fail, it makes you wiser, it makes you more aware, and when conceived the right way, it fuels you and makes you hungrier. Appreciate failure. Find comfort in uncomfortable situations, become immune to it. This is when you begin to attain all that God has for you.

By maturing in college and staying focused, it allowed me to realize that I needed to step out my comfort zone. I began to get more involved and speak out more. I accomplished so much and met a lot of great people who pushed me to do better.

God blessed me with an internship my freshman year, which isn't typical for freshmen. The internship was with the North Carolina Department of Transportation. This was a unique experience because I had the opportunity to take my grandparents to the governor's mansion for a reception, at the end of the program. My grandparents were born in the mid-1930s, therefore, they grew up in a time where the only black folk on the governor's property were maids and butlers. This was a very symbolic moment for them. There I realized that everything that I do is not for personal gain but for family.

Sacrifices are key!

"But as I looked at everything I had worked so hard to accomplish, it was all so meaningless—like chasing the wind. There was nothing really worthwhile anywhere."
-Ecclesiastes 2:11

Society blinds us of life, and we vaguely realize it. Shiny things are appealing, the allure of having a decent salary, a dope whip, *bloody shoes,* bragging right etc.—it's the American Dream; but is it your dream? We work extremely hard to attain these things, but why?

Scarface is one of my favorite movies of all time. The best scene is when Tony was at the fancy restaurant eating a five-star meal with his wife, living lavishly. He then began to question his success, what was the meaning behind it? There isn't one, it's almost like running on a treadmill, working extremely hard to get nowhere. This is mind boggling but it makes you rethink your perception of life. You can easily get caught up in that lifestyle and lose sight of your true purpose. A lot of people find value in the shiny things such as titles, money, etc. but honestly, it's all worthless!

While writing this book I studied the book of Ecclesiastes. Ecclesiastes to me is like Solomon's *Notes 2 Self.* Solomon, was the son of David, and was the richest man in the world, he had everything from women to rubies. Solomon also had something that was worth way more than all those materialistic things, wisdom! In Ecclesiastes he repeatedly indicates that everything in the world is meaningless, *like chasing the wind,* and when you think about it, it is. We all are going to the grave, right? So why do we do the things we do?

Everything reverts to purpose. Purpose is substance. Shiny thing blinds us of those hidden jewels.

What are those jewels? Wisdom! Wisdom showed Solomon that everything he had was useless. Wisdom guides purpose; it's like that of a contact lenses, it makes the vision clearer. All those jewels intertwine: wisdom, purpose, faith, passion and most importantly love. Yes, the allure is very enticing. People strive to be the king of the sandbox which is senseless. They fail to realize that the world is far greater than a sandbox, but complacency and fear rules their lives, so they stay in that box, pleasing a small crowd, but it isn't in lined with purpose, it's not authentic. J.Cole call em *False Prophets.*

Purpose is valuable because it takes all the meaningless shit in life and makes it meaningful, but it takes wisdom to truly understand that. Start to look at everything you do as a tool, to shine light. You must ask yourself, are you getting that job to get a check or are you trying to set up a path for the next person to show them that there is a way out. Purpose, is being able to leave a legacy. The world is ours but it's up to us how we take the ownership.

Some life lessons are indelible and stick like a scar that isn't going away. I remember a conversation I had with one of my mentors growing up, William Sherard. Will was speaking on purpose. The way he broke it down was different, but it was true. He said in life we are given three key elements: a purpose, a function, and a destiny.

Purpose is what we are called to do on this earth, our call of duty i.e. providing for your family, helping someone out their struggle, etc.

Functionality is your base, something you are very passionate about. My function is writing and philanthropy, being innovative to create opportunities for people.

Finally, your destiny is a combination of the two. The function serves as a machine fueled by purpose to construct your destiny.

Everyone's function is distinct, some people are dancers, others play ball, some are musically gifted, some paint portraits but they all serve a common goal— to translate a message. Muhammad Ali's function was boxing but through that he inspired so many people in some many different ways— this was his purpose in life and from that he reached his destiny. This gives our life meaning. We must fully understand our purpose and find what we are passionate about.

Another jewel that's more valuable than any materialistic thing on this earth is, our vision. I write about vision a lot in this book. Your vision is a guideline, it shows you things that God has in store for you in your life. You must believe in that vision and have the faith that you can accomplish what's seen in your inner thoughts. Everything you lay your eyes on, came from someone's vision. From your phone, to skyscrapers, all of it came from the vision or idea that someone had in the back of their head, they just believed in it. This is a powerful tool, that's how God created the heavens and the earth, from a vision!

When I wrote this piece, I witnessed the Carolina Panthers demolish the Arizona Cardinals in the 2015 NFC Championship, 49-15. Cam Newton had a groundbreaking game, throwing for 335 yards plus two rushing touchdowns, this has never been done in an NFC Championship game before. During the press conference, Cam was asked if he was shocked of his performance. His response, "No!" he went on to explain, "I've envisioned myself doing this on this same exact stage as a kid."

I'm a strong believer that if you see it, it can be done, but you must believe! Whatever it is your dreaming about, believe it and see yourself doing it, every day! Always remember faith without work is dead! Once you envision it, you must strategize to accomplish the things you see! God places visions in our lives for a reason.

VI

GOD'S WORD IS A MECHANISM THAT CONSTRUCT SIGHT; IT SHEDS LIGHT IN THE DARKEST AREAS IN OUR LIFE.

You may have heard of the ten percent in society or as W.E.B. Dubois called them, *The Talented Tenth.* Who are these individuals? What sets them apart from the rest of the population? They are risk takers, daredevils, those not afraid to fail. Now I'm not saying they will jump off a building and expect to land feet first, but they have the ambition and mentality to make that leap and risk everything.

Steve Harvey, is one of the most prominent comedians in the world. Steve quit his day job and began doing comedy full time. His friends thought he went crazy— *Why would you give up your only source of income to go broke and do comedy full time?* Steve took a chance, he believed in his dream so much, he gave up his job, to follow his dreams. This probably wasn't easy, it took a lot of faith, but had he not made that decision he wouldn't have been the Steve Harvey we know today. Steve is a daredevil, he went against the norms to pursue his vision. Sometimes this is what it takes to be successful.

In the Great book, the Father says, *all are called, but only* ***few*** *are chosen.* This breaks the people of the universe into two distinct categories *the called* and *the chosen.* How do you depict the two?

The moment that you are developed as a fetus in your mother's womb God encrypts your whole life, he gives you a purpose, unique gifts, and a detailed plan for your life. Therefore, he says, *all are called*; it's all for a greater purpose: to build his kingdom on this earth, to shed light on the dark areas for those who don't see their vision, it's a cycle. The problem, however, most of the called don't know they are chosen, some may realize, but are afraid to embrace their calling. This filters *the called* from *the chosen few,* the few being the ten percent.

The biggest barrier that prevents the called from being chosen, is fear. The chosen are the ten percent; they understand their duty, and everything that God encrypted them with to fulfill what they are called to do. The things that they do are most of the time abnormal, like when Steve left his job to do stand-up full time. Or Terrence J when he auditioned for 106 and Park in New York, didn't make the cut, and had to drive all the way to Atlanta for the next audition the following morning. You must embrace the narrow path to pursue your destiny, it's a rough road but it's worth it! Sounds cliché but that's it, it's that simple.

To be successful, you will encounter trials but you must put on the coats of endurance to embrace the winds of adversity as you travel the pathways of prosperity.

I had this conversation with one of my mentors, Christopher B. Leak, who is a senior financial advisor with Morgan Stanley. Chris shared with me a scripture:

Habakkuk 2:1-3

"I will climb up to my watchtower and stand my guard post. There I will wait to see what the Lord says and will answer my complaint. Then the Lord said to me "Write my answer plainly on tablets so that a runner can carry the correct message for others. This is a vision for a future time. It describes the end, it will be fulfilled. If it seems slow in coming, wait patiently, for it will surely take place. It will not be delayed."

When you discover your vision, you find wealth, it's valuable. Your vision produces life because it's encrypted by God—*The way, the truth, and THE LIFE.* Notice in the scripture, God didn't ask Habakkuk to look for his vision from a flat panel but on a watchtower, which indicates that his visions comes from a high place, it's profound. To find your vision sometimes it takes getting away from the world and going to your personal tabernacle where it's just you and God. God speaks through his many creations, it may not be direct, but he will surely send a sign that will communicate that vision to you.

With Joseph, he gave him the gift to interpret dreams, he showed him in his dreams that he would one day be the ruler over all of Egypt. Joseph was a Canaanite who was sold into slavery by his **twelve** brothers but him being enslaved led him to Egypt where he would eventually become King— all because of his dreams. Yes, he was tested but God made him a promise and by Joseph utilizing the gift God encrypted him with, he fulfilled his destiny.

Taking a leap, is challenging. Imagine standing on a cliff preparing to jump, granted you have a bungee cord attached to you but there is no guarantee that the bungee cord will remain stable, it could snap, and you could fall and get killed. Success isn't in where you land but in the jump, *the leap of faith*. You may fall but you had the fortitude to take the leap, sometimes that is all it takes, and God will provide the rest. We face the most fear right before the jump, but it's the daredevils who aren't afraid to leap and embrace everything that happens along the way, who encounter the most success.

Those daredevils are the Steve Jobs of the world, when he first pitched the Macintosh computer and was called insane. Or Shawn Carter when he started Rocafella Records after being rejected by endless record labels. Or Diddy when he founded Bad Boy Records, at 19 years old. Or my good man Robert F. Smith, who I had the pleasure of meeting, when Goldman Sachs let him go and he started Vista Equity Partners from ground zero. They didn't let fear or doubt interfere with making their jump. Yes, it can be fearful when you don't know what the outcome will be, you could fail, you could go broke, get turned down, etc. What makes you successful is taking that leap of faith no matter the outcome.

Don't just be called, be one of **The** chosen **FEW**

VII

"Don't let anyone think less of you because you are young. Be an example to all believers in what you say, in the way you live, in your love, your faith, and your purity." - 1 Timothy 4:12

The drive for me to be my own boss came my freshman year of college. Society preaches that you must be degreed, and have a seasoned background to start your own establishment. But that's not necessarily the case, the people in my circle went against the odds and took chances.

I met my business partner, Chinameze (Chin-nah-mez-zuh) Kelsey Okoro, the second semester of my freshman year. Kelsey was a young hustler from Nigeria and he saw that I was on my business shit too, so we instantly connected.

Kels pitched to me his business plan that he had been working on for like two years, Ram Connect. Ram Connect was a marketing service that bridged the gap between Winston-Salem State University and the Winston-Salem community by providing discounts and benefits for the school's population. I told him the concept was genius, especially with it impacting my city, I stressed to him *you got to move forward with this.* Kels explained that he's been trying but the university kept giving the runaround. A lot of the university's staff didn't believe in the concept because he was young.

Dr. Allen who had helped get me into school was ironically over the people who gave Kelsey the runaround. The following week I went to meet with Dr. Allen about the concept of Ram Connect, she loved it. Dr. Allen then met with Kelsey, I'm not sure what was discussed in the meeting, all I know is he never got the runaround again after they met. After that Kels asked me to join his team and things shot up from there.

A month after I joined Ram Connect, James Taylor, City Councilman for the City of Winston-Salem, another mentor of mine, caught the buzz of the moves we were making. Mr. Taylor set up an interview for us with the Chronicle, a local black newspaper. The Ram Connect Team was Kelsey, Kyle Brown, and myself. For us, this was huge, it felt like we were about to do an interview with Hot 97 or some shit. We had no idea what was going to spark from the interview.

When we got there, we met with Layla Garms, who was a journalist for the Chronicle; we conversed with Mrs. Garms for nearly an hour, the synergy in that room was so powerful. We talked about being black entrepreneurs in college and how we were trying to shift our culture. After we left the meeting she took a few photos of us downtown. I didn't know if we was going to be featured in the paper or what, she didn't say.

A couple of weeks passed, and we still didn't hear anything, I figured it would be a throw-a-way article. The Chronicle releases their papers every Thursday. One Thursday morning I decided to go to a local corner store to get the paper. I had a feeling we were going to be featured in that week's edition. When I walked in the store I seen the headline *Opportunity Knocks*— we were featured on the front fucking page! I couldn't believe it! I bought every copy. When I called Kels he thought I was playing so I sent him a picture. This was a remarkable feeling, it gave us hope. We were making a change! Opportunities do indeed knock.

Our first contractual agreement came shortly after that. Before the meeting Kels said he was going to let me pitch the deal. I never pitched a deal a day in my life, at least not on that level. But I went in there confident and determined. We negotiated a deal and signed our first contract with what was then Nitty Gritty, now Prime Tyme— a popular soul food restaurant in the city. The deal featured a twenty percent discount off all main entrees for the university's population! We closed multiple deals after that. The most valuable thing about it was everyone on campus was aware of the discounts but no one knew we were the face behind it, *the essence of moving in silence.*

Just because you're in college and young doesn't prevent you from taking over the world. You can create wealth for yourself AT ANY AGE! A lot of people are oblivious to that! We were those trailblazers, to show people that they can really do this shit. Take full advantage of the opportunities *that's knocking* at your door.

A lot of inspiration struck from Ram Connect. However, we decided to seize business my junior year. Kels had moved to Cali to pursue other endeavors including the launch of his first book *Dichotomy* which he released in January of 2016. For me, I was focused on finishing school. But it's a gem that we will always keep in our portfolio, you may hear about it again real soon!

There needs to be a revolution for black stake in America. When you go down the org chart, the wealthiest people in the world are dominated by foreigners. There are little to no African-Americans on the billionaire list, in fact, there are only three: Michael Jordan, Oprah Winfrey, and Robert F. Smith.

The Jews and Italians dominate the United States— from Corporate America to Silicon Valley.

Marcus Goldman was a Jewish immigrant who came to the United States in the late 19th century. Coming from nothing, Marcus founded Goldman Sachs, one of the largest banks in the world today. We need our own banks, tech firms, designer brands, all of that.

All it takes is taking that leap— you're going to encounter many obstacles along the way but it's all a part of the path. If we take those same core principles that Marcus Goldman had when he established

Goldman Sachs and create our own wealth, that would make a significant change in our economy and culture. You can be your **own boss**, and there is nothing wrong with that, it's a great feeling.

You develop leverage and freedom with no limitations when you're your own boss. Literally, any gift that you have you can turn it into a wealth generator. Not saying that it's all about the money, more so about the message, the legacy!

There's a difference between being wealthy and being rich. Anybody could be rich, not everyone can be wealthy. Wealth is leaving a footprint, a legacy behind for your family. You can win the lottery and become rich. Wealth has wisdom! Being able to spread your assets out, having royalties, trust funds, life insurance policies, wills, 401ks and retirement plans, to me that's wealth.

A deeper realm of generational wealth, is the beauty of utilizing your gifts that God encrypted you with, to create your own establishment and then passing that wealth down to your family. That's what the Jews did, that's what the Italians are doing, and that's how we need to do as well. There needs to be a push, somebody needs to trigger that **Alarm Clock.** We must wake up!

You ever wonder why Jewish people own all the property in America?

VIII

"In this game, the lesson's in your eyes to see
Though things change, the future's still inside of me"
-Tupac Shakur *Unconditional Love*

Losing a grandfather ain't easy. Especially right before you graduate college. My grandfather was a huge part of my life, he was one of the few individuals who could truly understand me, even when I was lost. Jack, wasn't my biological grandfather but blood couldn't have brought us any closer.

Papa, is what I called him, was one of the strongest soldiers I ever knew. Back in the day, he was a heavy smoker, he would go through multiple cigarette packs a day. In 2000, he had got ill because of his smoking habits. I was young at the time, so I couldn't really comprehend what was going on. Over the years his sickness got worst. Despite being ill, he was still a strong cat, he never showed his weakness.

Papa was a great golfer in his prime. He won several tournaments throughout the east coast and played at a least one course in most of the states throughout the country. He never went pro though, I think he enjoyed playing with his crew. My freshman year in college I began to pick up the sport and when I communicated that to my grandfather his soul lit up. Mind you he was very sick at the time, he could barely walk from the bedroom to the den without taking a breather, it was that serious! One day however he got up and took me out to the yard and showed me how to properly swing a golf club. This took a lot out of him but that shows how much he cared for me.

The older I got the closer me and my grandfather became. He kept it real with me about a lot of things, if something was on his mind he would call and talk to me about it. He was a diehard Panthers fan, as am I, on Sundays, I would invite him over to my apartment to watch the game with me. We were tight.

My junior year in college, I was in my night class; I received a missed call from my grandfather. When I called him back, he told me that he and granny had been in a bad car accident. I immediately went to the hospital after class.

A car ran a red light and smashed into the side of their vehicle causing their car to flip upside down, they were stuck for forty minutes before the ambulance came.

When I got to the hospital, Papa was still in the emergency room and they had taken my grandmother to another room. I went to visit my pops first. He was happy to see me when I walked in, he said: *we gonna be alright buddy.* He was strong. I could tell he was hurting but he would not show that weak side.

Senior year, was a different hustle for me. I was determined to graduate and get a job— I was pursuing to get to the *Rotten Apple*, Wall Street. Senior year was a tough year because I was picking up slack from my junior year— I had failed three courses. *Terrible right?* I told myself, however that I had to finish. I would've been the first in my immediate family to get a college degree in the first four years, so there wasn't another option.

The second semester of my senior year things began to pan out well, I had all the classes I needed to graduate, even snagged an internship with Morgan Stanley, a company that I ideally wanted to work for.

Everything was going good, then the 27th of February hit. This day already doesn't cope well with me because it is the day I lost my mother. I got a phone call that evening from my grandfather, he had been rushed to the hospital. My mood instantly changed, I began to think what if this was it, my mind started racing again. I went to visit him that night and he was positive about everything. I didn't understand how he did it after all that he had been through. Every day that he was in the hospital was a low day for me. One night he called and sounded as if he was suffering, I never heard him like this before. He told me "promise me you'll never smoke another cigarette! It's not worth it! I don't want anyone to have to experience what I'm going through right now!" I told him he had my word. That was my grandfather's first time ever exposing his weakness to me.

A few weeks before he went to the hospital, he did me a huge favor. I promised that I'd keep what he did between us, but I'll always cherish what he did, for the rest of my life. I feel like a person knows when it's their time.

My family is very dysfunctional, always have been. As a kid who lost his mother early on all I could ask for was a support system from my family, but that wasn't the case. My family, is like a shattered glass, broken and hard to put back together. That burns my soul because that's all my mother wanted, but you have to learn to live with the reality, I guess.

One evening I went to check up on my grandfather. He enjoyed my company, I was like his best friend. That evening my aunt's friend had been in a bad car accident and needed someone to come get her. My aunt called me but because I was with my grandfather it would have been a bit of a stretch for me to leave, so I told her I wasn't able to come. She was furious with me, but you can't be everyone's hero, it's impossible. *I ain't shit.* But I knew my grandfather needed me, so I felt no need to explain to her where I was.

About two weeks later my grandfather came home, although he didn't look like he was in a condition to leave but he was ready. They weren't treating him well at the retirement place that he was moved to after leaving the hospital, plus he just missed being home. The day he came back I went to visit him. He ain't look well at all. A few days later my grandmother told me that he hadn't been out of the bed since I came to visit, I began to get worried. And then that next morning, he passed away.

That numbness came back over me all over again. This time was different I was more mature, I had been in this situation before, but I still had a cold heart. Now two of the closest people to me were gone. I began to ask myself why do I have to continue to lose loved ones, I felt isolated. My family wasn't making it any better either. You start to see how people maneuver during a death, they'll put greed over grief.

My aunt still wasn't rocking with me after my grandfather passed because she felt like I was wrong for not helping her that day she needed me. I understood where she was coming from completely, I just didn't like how she went about the whole situation. All this just adds to the pain. But I told myself that life ain't stopping for nobody, I had to keep moving forward.

A week after my grandfather passed, I got a message on Instagram saying that my roommate from my freshman year was killed, my heart was completely heavy. This kid had the world ahead of him, I remember conversations we had our freshman year about life and taking over and just like that he was gone. He was supposed to be walking that stage with me the following month. As much as I wanted to, I couldn't give up. God gives the toughest battles to his strongest soldiers, therefore I had to stay strong, giving up wasn't an option.

The battle isn't easy, you must have the endurance of a warrior. You might lose some people along the way, some people will turn their back on you, others might laugh at you, but you can let none of that stop you! Meek Mill said it's the price of being great! You gon have some wins and you gon suffer some loses but you got to push forward no matter what! Only the strong survive!

I miss my people every day, but I know they are looking down on me from above so I'm going to live my life to the fullest!

Rest in Peace Shayne. Rest in Peace Daryl B. Shamiyah Rest Easy. Long Live Lee! Krishon may your soul rest peacefully my brother. Celeste keep peace my love, I pray God has a basketball court for you up there! Rest in Peace Papa and to your brother Uncle Jim, Rest Easy! Ma rests easy baby!!

Papa,

I still can't believe you ain't here anymore playa. Life getting real. Don't really know who to trust anymore. You were like the last real one left. But listen I write this to let you know that I appreciate everything you did for me, you always were there. When you left this earth, I ain't want to believe it, I thought you was going to live forever! I didn't have the strength to speak at your funeral, my soul was too weak. You were one of the closest people to me, you showed me life, and how to be a man. I can't thank you enough for being a part of my life! You not suffering anymore my g, probably up there at a Marvin Gaye concert with the butterfly collar and the parachute pants on, jamming! Your grandson going through right now but I'm staying strong just like you always taught me. I haven't really talked to anybody from the family since you left, heart been too cold, and I've been focused. Tell my ma I said "Hey, ma!" haha. Love you papa know you're always going to be remembered OG, I'm dedicating this book to you, Jack!!

Q

"Never allow your journey to impair your vision!"
-Darrell Q,. Slade

God gives me these crazy visions all the time, as he does with all his children. I'm just ludicrous enough to believe that they are true, well it's not ludicrous its faith. The greatest vision God gave me thus far was when I was eighteen. I feel like he had been trying to deliver this vision to me for years I just didn't comprehend it until then. This vision gave me hope and a drive, it set me apart. The vision was bright, he called me to be a modern-day prophet, a ruler over my own empire! The world is ours, and I believe that.

God said to me *I am the first and the last. My own hand laid the foundations of the earth, and my right hand spread out the heavens.* **Isaiah 48: 12-13**

God is the movie director, he knows the full script, you're just in one scene right now!

I kept this vision to myself for a long time, it was true to me, I didn't feel a need to exploit it. A lot of people do things just to boast, there isn't any substance behind what they do, it's not true to them but it feels good. I believe that's where I messed up.

When you have something special ahead of you it's so easy to get distracted. The devil is trying to entice you away from your vision. Sometimes you'll get distracted and not even know it and that's scary.

One of the organizations I joined during my college career was the Student Investment Fund, *Ram Asset Management, LLC.* The fund was great, it gives students the opportunity to learn about the stock market and have hands-on experience with investing real liquid assets. This exposed me to *the jungle*, Culprit

America! The fund was invaluable, it taught me the essence of investing and managing money, which can carry you a long way. A lot of doors began to open for me during my time with the fund. I learned how much brokers on Wall Street made and was intrigued— I wanted that lifestyle!! I had to make it to the street, and I'm not talking crack fiends and drug dealers, even though the biggest drug fiends that you never hear about, are on Wall Street.

From there my grind shifted. I went to a conference in New York and I saw all these corporate gurus in their fancy suits, living this corporate lifestyle, I was thrilled. I was thinking the whole time *I had to make it here*, this boosted my ego. I began to come up with a strategic plan to get to Wall Street.

My sophomore year I interned with Piedmont Investment Advisors, a hedge fund out of Durham, North Carolina. A hedge fund is an investment fund that pools capital from accredited individuals and institutions and invests their assets in a diversified portfolio. At piedmont I witnessed a stock broker from New York execute a trade for the firm over the phone— this was wicked, he probably made a thousand dollars off that one transaction. This made me more determined to go corporate. *Shiny things are blinding.*

The second semester of my senior year in college, I interned with Morgan Stanley. Morgan Stanley is one of the top financial institutions in the United States. For me this was huge, I had come a long way. There weren't too many people where I'm from that went corporate, I felt accomplished. Not to mention I was the only African-American in the whole office aside from my mentor Chris Leak, who granted me the internship. I was the first intern from an HBCU to work in that local office, it was an honor. For those unaware an HBCU is a Historically Black College and University. I felt like a pioneer blazing a path for my people to follow.

Chris saw that hustle ambition in me, he saw that I was determined to make it in this industry. We had multiple conversations about being of color in a corporate office. It puzzled me. These corporate companies want to become more diverse, yet you have to "suit-up" to their culture to blend in. Dare not to be yourself, that's not acceptable. But I wanted to make a change, I wanted to be able to be myself and still make it corporate.

Ultimately, this was yielding me away from my vision. One of the things I discussed with Chris was my plan to one day have my own business. He explained to me OBI, a regulation by the Securities Exchange Commission (SEC). OBI stands for outside business interest, this limits you from developing your own business if you are employed by a fiduciary institution. I heard this and my mind was blown but I was kind of like fuck it I'm still going to go corporate! *Never allow your journey to impair your vision!* My short-term goal, was to go corporate for a while then start my own business after I gained enough experience.

In May of 2017, I graduated from Winston-Salem State University with a Bachelor of Science as a Finance

Major. For me this was huge because everyone doubted me along the way and no one expected me to even get into college. I had worked extremely hard to get that degree and I accomplished so much throughout my college career. I knew my mother would have been proud of me; I came a long way since she left this earth. My mom proclaimed everything would be alright before she left, and everything was coming in to order. But then I had to face reality, life after graduation.

I had three career opportunities after I graduated: work full-time for Nationwide in Columbus, OH, a financial advisor program with Edward Jones in St. Louis, MO, or pursue a career with Morgan Stanley. I really wanted to work for Morgan Stanley, but I don't believe Morgan Stanley wanted me to work for them. Every time I applied for a full-time position, I got *This position is closed until next year* or *I don't think that position is available*— the run around.

The application process with Edward Jones took forever and went well into the summer, so I ended up taking the Nationwide opportunity which I had secured in February. I figured I'd work there until something else came up.

To be honest, I was afraid to embrace my destiny that God had for me, I put it on the back burner. I contradicted everything I said in this book up until this point, I pivoted away from the vision to chase materialistic shit! I fell into that corporate system and got distracted. *House nigga!*

When I got to Ohio I was a bit conceded, I'll be honest. I had just left one of the top banks in the world to work at an insurance company, in internal audit. Keep in mind, Nationwide is a Fortune 500 company, but it wasn't Morgan Stanley. The vibe was off for me, a lot of the people there was complacent. I felt like everyone was on a treadmill *working extremely hard to get nowhere*— Sound familiar? This is when I began to realize that this corporate America shit wasn't for me. I mean if I was destined for the top, why was I settling? There's no way you can make it to the top when you're in a system, especially corporate. Not only was this on my mind but I was away from my family and I had just lost my grandfather, I was stressed out. This impacted my performance in the workplace, I didn't know shit about internal audit, I was just there to collect a check at that point. On top of that, I found out that I didn't get the Edward Jones position. Could anything else go wrong?

My mind was running. I kept thinking *Here I am giving Nationwide forty hours a week but what am I gaining in return though? Brownie Points? A Salary? Maybe a raise?*

None of this was in line with my purpose, I was *chasing the wind.* All the work that I was contributing to the firm flows into their enterprise to make them shine even brighter. God kept telling me *I have something greater for you!* All I could think about was me running my own business, and accumulating self-wealth! If I dedicated the time I gave corporate to construct my own foundation, I would one day have my own "Nationwide" or "Morgan Stanley".

Well, my piss poor performance on the job showed. It wasn't like I was doing terrible shit, I was getting my work done I just struggled to adapt. I got called out for yarning and showing up late for meetings. One of my favorites, I had been told "I wasn't capable of using excel" because I raised the question "how do you add a column on a spreadsheet" in a meeting. I mean it was ridiculous, but I take ownership, I didn't work to the best of my ability.

I was fed up, it felt like I was a target, I was getting called out for every little thing I did. I went to express my concerns with a lady who was over all the new employees and interns. I told her I didn't like the environment and she was very understanding; she told me that she was going to see if she could move me to a different department.

The next morning, I got called into a meeting, I figured I was about to get moved to a different department. Present in the meeting was my supervisor, the lead auditor, the Assistant Vice President for internal audit, and the lady whom I met with the day prior. During the meeting each of the participants went on a rant about how piss poor my performance was. I felt like I was getting jumped, I honestly didn't know the purpose of the meeting anymore, I just let them have it, at that point I was used to it.

This went on for nearly forty-five minutes. The lady who I met with the day before then told me that it was best for them to let me go! At first, I was puzzled because just the day before she reasoned with me saying she would help me. Yet all I could do was smile, I felt no reason to release the rage I had boiling inside, instead I told them *thank you.* This was needed, I was now free. This opened a door for me to get back on the path that God originally called me down. We all take blows in life but no matter what we have to push forward.

I can't lie this hurt. As I left the building, I came across a homeless man. He asked me the typical question most homeless people ask, "you have any change?" I responded, "No! All I have is my card," he said “well we can walk to an ATM”. When I told him, I had been fired, he asked me to give him a hug, and I did. The guy told me to ask him "excuse me, sir?". When I asked he ignored me. He then went on to say, "Thousands of people walk out that office every day and walk right past me as if I’m not here or I’m deaf". He told me that he appreciated me for having the courage to talk to him about what happened. This was profound, it made me think back to purpose. If a candle is in a lit area it serves no purpose, but if you take that same candle to a dark area it begins to fulfill its destiny, to shed light. You must be humble!

The devil is in a spiritual war with God. He wants to take away your light as much as he can because God's light is so powerful. You must have wisdom to understand that. The devil tries to distract you from your light and he does it in a distinct way. It's like fool’s gold, he's going to paint a vision too, just like how God is doing. He's going to byte what God does and entice you, but that vision is not leading to where God is trying to lead you. It's the pathway for destruction. This is what he did with Jesus when he took him to the mountaintop and showed him all the kingdom's in the world and told him that it could all be his, IF he bowed down to him. But Jesus had great wisdom and discernment, he knew his duty was to remain faithful to God.

That kingdom for me was Corporate America, the devil painted that picture nice; here he'll give me a substantial salary, a nice home, great benefits, entitlement, power— *those shiny things*. Really what he was doing was blinding me, taking me away from what God had for me. This will dim your light, that is the devil's plan. When God sees that, he will begin to close doors along that path, as a sign. If you don't have understanding, you would look at a closed door as a failure, *maybe I'm not worthy enough to travel this path*. What God is trying to tell you is *this is not the path I destined for you! Turn around and follow me!*

Isaiah 48:20-21

20 Leave Babylon, flee from the Babylonians! Announce this with shouts of joy and proclaim it. Send it out to the ends of the earth; say, "the Lord has redeemed his servant Jacob." 21 They did not thirst when he led him through the deserts; he made water flow for them from the rock; he split the rock and water gushed out

Wisdom is indicative because without wisdom you can't have that spiritual ear to understand what's going on. When I lost my job, that was God trying to tell me *Son I didn't want you to go do that! Do you not see?! I want you to inherit your own grain, I want you to start your own enterprise, this is what I have been telling you all alone. Build your own kingdom within my kingdom because you are me and I am in you, so you are destined to have a kingdom because I have a kingdom!*

We all have kingdoms because we are all God's children— Gods of the Earth. Protect yourself from the distractions of the world, all it is, is the devil trying to conquer your kingdom. A distraction grows the devil's profit. It's like a business, trying to stop their competitor from growing, and that's all the devil is trying to do. The only competitive advantage the devil has is the lackluster individuals here on this earth who have fallen into his trap.

If God says we have everything, why limit yourself? Limitation grows the devil's dynasty because one doesn't understand and has a lack of wisdom. That's why it's essential for us to use these flashlights that God has equipped us with to shine that light to show his people that they can step outside that box! Stay true to your divine path!

Words From Kwa'tre Hollingsworth, IV

IV is like family to me, we practically grew up together. Two years ago when I began writing the book, we met up during our Winter Break, he had just finished his first semester at Howard. When we got up, IV ironically told me that he was about to drop a book. This caught me by surprise because from our city you don't see kids dropping books, especially not at nineteen, and on top of that his intellect was on a whole different level! I decided to share a poem from his Book "Through These Eyes", entitled '9-5'. This poem is very relatable to the message from the previous chapter.

9-5

Kwa'tre Hollingsworth, IV

Up with the sun just to be on time

7:00 just to make it at 9

Hopped on the bus and a metro train ride

Just to make it to my 9 to 5

Working for the government when I really don't be feeling the Feds

Spending all these billions

then I look out the office window
People sleeping on the side walk
What a struggle life they live
Then I think
What if I had no belongings?
No material things
Would I still have to fight the evil the world brings?
Would God still be making my heart sing?
Without this green
Without this 9 to 5 would I feel alive?
If I slept on the concrete with no worries would I stress over anything?
Out of these thousands of people that pass by
Somebody will see the hurt in these eyes
Somebody will buy me a meal
All I would have to do is find a place to sleep on these streets
Be happy and somebody gone give to this meek
Just gone pray to God it ain't bad weather this week
9 to 5 working for the man
I don't really like this shit

Just learning from the experience
I never followed Uncle Sam
I thought I was already the man
9 to 5 and it's only week two and I'm ready to bounce
Gotta make some moves, time to let the lion out
I'm going to get it, look at this predators pounce
Look at this 9 to 5, the money me but this ain't me
The money me, I got a dream business plan for the kids
Time to bounce, a lion can't be truly tamed.
Fuck a 9 to 5 I'm out.
You gone remember my name

Excerpt from *Through These Eyes* Available on Amazon.

This the letter from my mother

Son,

I knew you was going to shine! Even when I saw you in Atlanta, I knew! You wasn't even born yet. The doctors was telling me *you can't have no baby! You too old*! *Your tubes tied*! God was like *You got a son and he gone shine!* You are like the golden child! You are a miracle to the world young boy! And even though I'm gone—I am still with you!

I'm talking to you through spirit. Yea son, you live through me but we living through God, it's a legacy, keep it all in the family! Let your light shine! Don't be scared, that's only the devil, he's saying *no, you can't do that*! but like God did, he gave birth and I'm true to that!

You my son baby boy, trust, I'm with you. Stay strong, keep your head up! Life is tough, life is rough, but it's all a part of the plan that God made for you baby!

Yeah this your mother, talking to you from heaven. God right behind me and he's affirming everything I'm saying baby!

Be a family man! Don't get lost! Have self-control and discipline. That's how I taught you, charm and etiquette, you remember that!

You my baby boy, my prize possession! I said *everything was going to be alright* before I left this earth, because God was telling *me Ima give your son faith*; *Ima give him endurance to survive the dark storms!*

You my pride and joy! I see you writing your book, you got God's words all in it! Everything that I invested in you is coming to life! I saw it happening! This is why I told you, I'm proud of you, that day in the hospital room. I remember when you held my hand and read me Galatians 5:22, baby boy that got me through!

I was strong in the flesh! When they removed my breast, I had to stay strong for you!

This your mother talking through you. This my letter to you! I love you. Tell your brother I love him too! Y'all got each other, that's beautiful! Don't get emotional, cause I'm with you! I'm in spirit channeling my life through you!

You my baby boy, you was destined to be born. They said no but God had a divine purpose for you! This my letter to my son. This my letter to the world!

Keep wisdom, faith and dignity – *Proverbs 3 verse 22*, that's for you Q! I knew you was going to find it, God led you that way, it was divine, the spiritual way! Read that, take heed to that! I'm talking to you in spirit.

You my son, my pride and joy! Write this down so you can always enjoy— your mother talking to you from heaven, son. I love you!

Signed,

Heaven's Angel

Childhood
Written by Darrell Q. Slade

Physically I can't go back, time machines don't exist, but I gotta go so I write– back to my childhood. Cox Blvd, My mother's presence seizes the room. Listening to Maya Angelou brings her aroma back to me. Her smile lights the night, made Winston-Salem feel like a piece of Harlem. The culture marinates the atmosphere. My my, I'm only three so I can't really think but I feel her love for me. In between clients she coming to hold me, near and dear nowhere else I'd rather be. Mmhmm. Writing brings me back, like a time machine. **Letter from Ma** *is my mother writing to me; she's here so go back with me. Early on, gray days just me and mommy! Wooden chairs old classic TV. Vintage days was the best for me. Beautiful what the spirit does– bringing back old memories. Miss them old days, gravel driveway, big ole tree. Don't know if this poetry but it brought me– back to them days with me and my mommy. Death bestowed them days from me. Spirit from with inside taking me on a journey. Miss that ole salon cement steps to my mother's* **place of beauty***! Back to them days when it was just me and mommy. Maya reminds me of* *her, the epitome of Darrell Louise. Remember when she kept me, Delacy, and Demitri. Bring me back to them days of my mommy. Thoughts locked in my mind God let them free– I really just want to see them times I spent with my mommy. Think of old vintage thrifts filled with dashikis. God's greatest gift was the fourteen years with my mommy. She's in an enclosed glass tryna get through to me, seeing everything, lord help me. I know she happy cause she reading me, world don't understand, but she know her baby. Back seat in the Mercedes watching my mommy. This love too good to be true so God took her from me. Early morning, mother on the phone voice sweet as honey. Time machines supernatural– I'm back with my mommy! Running round lost because I lost my mommy. Going back to the time when my brother had the flat top fade– he upset cause ma last name changed to Slade, hated my father, but look what they made– a boy who would be scared indefinitely. Wish the laws of life wasn't true to me because I would go back in time and be with my mommy. God's understanding is far too complex for me. Bring me back to the days when she surprised me. Heart so warm never felt the cold days. Just sitting here listening to Maya made me think of my mommy; she did her hair, wonder what conversations they had– maybe that synergy is what inspired me to write like a caged bird. My mother's presence is inside me. Keeps me sane in this world that's so crazy. Jlysa brought me back made me think– young Kimmy, seen her the other day but she don't remember me, Jackie was home her husband worked on PCs. Mrs. Oxly in the shop giving me books to read. Lord take me back to them old days cause I miss my mommy.*

Your words and spirit will forever live through me ma.

I love you always.

Your son, *the golden child.*

For I am about to do something new. See, I have already begun! Do you not see it? I will make a pathway in the wilderness. I will create rivers in the dry wasteland. -Isaiah 43:19

Everybody not going to see that vision! They not going to support you. They will call you crazy when you pursue your vision because you're going against the odds, doing *the impossible.*

God says he about *to do a new thing*— Isaiah 43:19. Being new is abnormal, so of course, people are going to doubt it. But if God planned it then its destined to happen and it will change your life for the better!

The devil tries to throw critics in the way as a distraction. He places those doubters in your life to blind you; he wants you to believe what they say.

Staying true to what you believe is key even if the whole world is against you. You must be willing to die for what you believe, that's true faith.

You can't fall into society's trap but believe what God is whispering in your ear. The narrow path is a challenge but that's only to prevent those worthy of travel from the multitude. Therefore, be ready for the ride and keep fortitude along the way. Most of all enjoy the journey because it's all for the better! Whether you lose a mother, get fired from a job, or battle with rejection— it's all a part of God's plan!

Had not those things happened to me, I wouldn't have the drive that I have now; I wouldn't have any fuel because I would be complacent so therefore my fuel would be useless. Stay away from complacency in every form. Instead, allow your struggles to be the fuel to drive your ambition to accomplish your vision, your promised land, that goal you had your whole life!

When you reach the top of the mountain and

fulfilled your destiny, that alarm will ring so loud that it will wake your enemies, who've slept on you for so long!

Move quietly until you've reach the top, that's when your dignity is produced. This is *the true essence of moving in silence!*

This book is special to me because it gives a pure form of my emotions, thoughts, feelings, ideas, etc. I really enjoy the art of writing; today's society is taking away from the authenticity of art due to the advancement of technology, which is a gift and a curse. However, this whole book, start to finish, was written by hand, word for word, in a notebook I found in my apartment.

Letter from Ma was the only chapter that wasn't written, originally. God has a unique way of communicating to his children; Letter from Ma was a voice note, I recorded on my phone— each word flowed out beginning to end, persistently. This was nothing but God. I was really amazed how it happened and I truly believed that it was a heavenly message sent from my mother. I decided to add it as a chapter in my book because it puts everything in perspective. After I spoke this piece, I felt it was only necessary for me to scribe it in my journal and it is something that I will always cherish and keep forever.

As mentioned in the prologue, I didn't want to write a book at first, so when I first began writing, it was challenging for me to flow my thoughts on paper. But the more I wrote the more I enjoyed writing. This was an on and off process for nearly a year before I began the publishing stages. I may add that this book wasn't written in order, in fact chapter four, *Promised Land,* was the first chapter written— the original title for the chapter was the Power of Circumcision. The chapters where I open up about my mom were the hardest for me to write because I always kept that pain hidden, this is my first time really opening up about those moments. I see kids, like myself, losing their mothers daily— I had to be vulnerable. Know, we are not alone and God still loves us and has bigger plans for our lives though nothing can replace our mothers.

I didn't come up with the name The Alarm Clock until halfway through the written process— it was one of those supernatural moments where I knew it was the perfect fit. A lot of things flow from The Alarm Clock. A clock is a cycle, there is a time for everything as Solomon referenced in Ecclesiastes— a time for rest, and a time to wake up. It was time for me to write this novel because it's time for us to wake up. Never miss out on your time!

An alarm clock is one of the most silent devices, until its activated! The sole purpose of an alarm clock is to wake a person up. For me an alarm clock symbolizes purpose. When you are walking in purpose, you don't walk amongst the crowd, you move silently because your every move doesn't require sound. Nowadays you have a lot of noise makers who tend to get attention from the crowd, they are trying to wake an audience who is already woke, therefore their alarm serves no purpose. But those who walk silently in their purpose will eventually awaken those who have been sleep!

This book is my alarm clock to the world. My people are sleep— it's time for us to wake up and inherit the land that's promised to us. We have to shift our thought process as we wake up.

When you are sleep, your eyes are closed, therefore you can't *see* what's in front of you. God called me to open the eyes of those who are resting, and show them they can accomplish anything that they put their minds towards; it sounds cliché but it's *the truth*!

I am here to wake those who slept on me! When you move silently people will indeed sleep on you, cherish those who sleep on you. My grandmother always reminds me that if you tell everyone your business you won't have none. Continue to move silently and the world will surely see your work. I've always stayed quiet about the moves that I made, I barely told anyone that I was writing this book. You'll find that the things that you remain humble about will be the most profound when its revealed to the world.

When you hear your alarm go off in the morning, typically, you don't want to wake up, most people want to lay around longer because they don't believe that it's their time to get up but you can't deny the truth! When your alarm goes off the people who've slept the longest aren't going to want to wake up because they are complacent and in a comfortable place.

Growth is produced from change, but you can't change when you're in a comfortable position it's not going to work. Comfortability is a weapon of mass destruction that the devil uses against the holy.

To grow you must get up when your alarm sounds, and step out your comfort zone. The hardest part about waking up in the morning is getting out the bed but once you get up you gain a spark of energy. You must discipline yourself to be comfortable outside your comfort zone. Once you begin to operate in uncomfortable climates your faith begins to develop, and you will start accomplishing things that you never imagined.

The biggest inspiration from this book came from my mother: her words, her wisdom, her spirit, all these things will forever live through me. Losing her was the toughest thing I had to encounter. I wrote this book for that next kid who lost a loved one or going through a similar struggle; showing them that they can use their pain and conquer the world!

One morning I was at my apartment, I got a phone call from my pops: he had left his cellphone at the house and wanted me to bring it to his job. My apartment was on the opposite side of town and the house was another twenty minutes away from his job. As much as I didn't feel like doing this, I had to be obedient. When I got to the house, I discovered my mother's applicable bible. My mother was a woman of faith, she had all types of footnotes in almost every page of her bible. I always enjoy flipping through those notes in her bible.

When I picked up the bible, the first page I flipped to was Proverbs the third chapter, there I noticed a bracket that noted *For Quentin*, (Quentin is my middle name) dated March 31, 2008 around the time she first got sick. The scripture reads

Proverbs 3:21-28 NIV

21 *My son, do not let wisdom and understanding out of your sight, preserve sound judgment and discretion;* ***22*** *they will be life for you, an ornament to grace your neck.* ***23*** *Then you will go on your way in safety, and your foot will not stumble.* ***24*** *When you lie down, you will not be afraid; when you lie down, your sleep will be sweet.* ***25*** *Have no fear of sudden disaster or of the ruin that overtakes the wicked,* ***26*** *for the LORD will be at your side and will keep your foot from being snared.* ***27*** *Do not withhold good from those to whom it is due, when it is in your power to act.* ***28*** *Do not say to your neighbor, "Come back tomorrow and I'll give it to you"— when you already have it with you.*

Excerpts from Letter from Ma: *Keep wisdom, faith and dignity— Proverbs 3 verse 22, that's for you Q! I knew you was going to find it, God led you that way, it was divine, the spiritual way!*

When I found this, I was in awe! This was surely my mother talking to me. Had I not gone to the house that day I probably would have never found those words. God works in mysterious ways and I believe that he destined for me to find that bible. What was miraculous, that scripture was consistent with the words throughout this book and the core values I developed since the death of my mother.

This book is truly a huge accomplishment for me. I learned a lot about myself throughout the process. I had no idea that I had the gift of writing until I put the pen to the paper. I will say however transcribing your truest thoughts, feelings, and emotions is not an easy task.

As you might know this book has twelve chapters,

that's intentional. An alarm clock has twelve hours in it, therefore every chapter is a representation of each hour on the clock. On a more complex level my target audience are the youth in the city that I'm from, Winston-Salem, North Carolina. The nickname for Winston-Salem is the *Tre-Fo* or *3-4*. Three **times** four is twelve, it's a *hidden jewel*! The alarm clock is set to directly wake the people in my city up but indirectly wake everyone in the world up.

One night, I was flying out to Dallas, Texas for a conference. I had a layover in Denver. As I was in route to Denver I was in a peaceful mind state. I planned to do some edits for my book during my layover which was about four and a half hours. I heard God speak to me on the flight, he asked me to listen to the audio version of Ecclesiastes as I was working on my edits, so I did. I mention Ecclesiastes in the earlier chapter *Hidden Jewels*.

Ecclesiastes is such a powerful novel, when I played it at the airport I had to stop working, just to listen what Solomon was saying. I listened to the entire book that night in the airport. When I finished the final chapter, God revealed to me: *The Book of Ecclesiastes also had twelve chapters*! My mind was completely blown. This was a reassurance! I am not sure of the message that God was trying to tell me, but it was indeed valuable.

I pray my story will shine a light so bright in your life that it will light up pathways that you never knew existed. This book is not for individual accreditation but a tool to expand the kingdom of God here on this Earth. Shalom.

Acknowledgements

The biggest influence for this project came from God, the father. God communicates to me through his many creations. I'm just glad I can interpret the messages and share it with you, the world. I believe this is why he called me to write this book. None of these words are my words and none of the experiences I went through in life were unintentional, they all served a purpose, to transcend inspiration. This is my first piece of literature, I never in a million years thought that I would see the day where I'd write a book. It's amazing what God will do for you if you are obedient. I take no credit in this literature, ALL GOD.

Corvaya Jeffries, Journalist. I'm all for elevation and expansion therefore I asked her to be my editor. I'm honored to have partnered with her for this project to say the least. Much Love.